Parenting Toddlers

Teaching Children With Logic to Raise Happy and Successful Kids

(A Grown-up's Guide to Getting Over Emotionally Immature Parents)

David Gordon

Published by Rob Miles

© **David Gordon**

All Rights Reserved

Parenting Toddlers: *Teaching Children With Logic to Raise Happy and Successful Kids (A Grown-up's Guide to Getting Over Emotionally Immature Parents)*

ISBN 978-1-990084-27-0

All rights reserved. No part of this guide may be reproduced in any form without permission in writing from the publisher except in the case of brief quotations embodied in critical articles or reviews.

Legal & Disclaimer

The information contained in this book is not designed to replace or take the place of any form of medicine or professional medical advice. The information in this book has been provided for educational and entertainment purposes only.

The information contained in this book has been compiled from sources deemed reliable, and it is accurate to the best of the Author's knowledge; however, the Author cannot guarantee its accuracy and validity and cannot be held liable for any errors or omissions. Changes are periodically made to this book. You must consult your doctor or get professional medical advice before using any of the suggested remedies, techniques, or information in this book.

Upon using the information contained in this book, you agree to hold harmless the Author from and against any damages, costs, and expenses, including any legal fees potentially resulting from the application of any of the information provided by this guide. This disclaimer applies to any damages or injury caused by the use and application, whether directly or indirectly, of any advice or information presented, whether for breach of contract, tort, negligence, personal injury, criminal intent, or under any other cause of action.

You agree to accept all risks of using the information presented inside this book.

You need to consult a professional medical practitioner in order to ensure you are both able and healthy enough to participate in this program.

Table of Contents

INTRODUCTION 1

CHAPTER 1: HOW TO KNOW YOU ARE READY? 2

CHAPTER 2: TYPES OF PARENTING STYLES 8

CHAPTER 3: ON REALISM, PRACTICALITY, AND DETERMINATION 14

CHAPTER 4: DE-GADGETIZING YOUR CHILD 19

CHAPTER 5: ADVICE FOR PARENTING DYSLEXIC CHILD IN CLASSROOM 32

CHAPTER 6: STRATEGIES THAT WORK 42

CHAPTER 7: LEARN TO SAY NO 48

CHAPTER 8: HOW TO END SIBLING RIVALRY: HOW TO REACT AND WHAT TO DO WHEN YOUR CHILDREN START FIGHTING 55

CHAPTER 9: LEARN TO LET GO 67

CHAPTER 10: SAFE AND FUN OUTDOOR ACTIVITIES FOR KIDS DURING SUMMER 73

CHAPTER 11: IMPORTANCE OF A CLEAN, SAFE HOME LIFE 81

CHAPTER 12: WHEN FAMILY PROBLEMS COME 94

CHAPTER 13: HOW TO HANDLE TEMPER TANTRUMS 105

CHAPTER 14: ADVICE FROM PARENTS 115

CHAPTER 15: LABOR AND BIRTH 120

CHAPTER 16: TOP POSITIVE PARENTING QUALITIES ALL PARENTS SHOULD POSSESS 133

CHAPTER 17: DO NOT SET YOUR EXPECTATIONS TOO HIGH 144

CHAPTER 18: POSITIVE PARENTING WITH YOUNG CHILDREN 148

CHAPTER 19: IN A NUTSHELL 153

CHAPTER 20: DON'T PROGRAM YOUR CHILD WITH NEGATIVE RUBBISH 166

CHAPTER 21: COMMUNICATION AND ENVIRONMENT .. 170

CHAPTER 22: FIXING A CHILD'S BEHAVIOR 175

CHAPTER 23: MAKE THEM FEEL SPECIAL AND LOVED 182

CHAPTER 24: SOFTWARE RECOMMENDATION FOR CHILDREN OF DIFFERENT AGES 187

CONCLUSION 192

Introduction

Sound familiar? Probably. In a world of parenting guru's, do's and do not's it's hard to find the most effective parenting style. A seasoned behavioral counselor gives insight to easy to maneuver tactics that downright work in an effective and fast acting guide that will hit on common parenting pitfalls and how to immediately turn them around.

This guide was created with the busy and cooperative parent in mind. You have little time to read lengthy textbooks or other resources, you need something that is effective and works quickly, and you have the commitment to make sure you follow through.

Chapter 1: How To Know You Are Ready?

Parenting is a full-time job. It comes with its own set of responsibilities and is not at all easy. Being a single parent is a challenge in itself. Women become single parents due to many reasons. Some choose to be so while some are single mothers by chance like death of a spouse or divorce or other such reasons.

The decision to become a single mother is therefore at times a well-deliberated one and sometimes it happens by a stroke of destiny.

Whatever be the reason, it becomes absolutely necessary to raise your children in the best manner possible.

At the same time, you need to ensure that you do not lose yourself as a person, while being a single parent.

Here are some simple tips to ensure you are ready to take the role of a single mother.

Be emotionally prepared:

The most important prerequisite of being a single mother is finding whether you have the emotional stability to bring a child into the world. It also applies if you have to raise a child by yourself, in case you choose to adopt one. Raising a child can be both scary and liberating. You need to be emotionally ready to take up the job because once you take a decision; there is no option of backing out.

Motherhood is a huge responsibility and it is a tough world to survive in. Therefore, be absolutely sure of your decision and avoid emotional vulnerability at all times.

In divorce cases, there are two things one is required to fight. On one hand, you have to cope with the pain of falling out with your spouse. On the other hand, you have to take up the responsibility of the child / children at the same time.

The death of a spouse is perhaps a major setback and a real nightmare. The worst part is that you are thrown into a crisis without being mentally prepared. Emotional and mental strength is the most important prerequisite in handling such an unfortunate incident.

Learn to depend but not completely rely on others:

Establish a support system of people who are compassionate and supportive of your decision and at the same time, ignore people who are critical. Being a single parent can be stressful sometimes. You may feel emotionally drained to do a job, which is typically a couple's job. It is thereby important that you surround yourself with supportive people that you can fall back on.

There will be people who would jump to every chance they get to show you down. Keep away from such people or completely ignore them.

Be financially independent:

Looking at family or friends for support is a good idea but not always, especially when it comes to finances. In fact, finances should be worked out so that you do not become a liability upon anyone.

Here are a few steps that can help you deal in a better manner with your finances:-

Prioritise responsibilities: This basically means a better work and family life management. A single mother has to take care of the house, the job, the bills and the children at the same time. All of this requires excellent management skills and setting and achieving long and short term goals.

Budgeting becomes crucial as you will have to take decisions based on the circumstances. A realistic budget, with some amount set aside for unforeseen situations will help to manage finances better. It also ensures a smooth tension-free life.

Insurance is necessary to protect your future and also is instrumental in dealing with accidents or illnesses.

Plan your child's education in advance and set aside funds for the same. In the beginning, you might have to cut down on your expenses. Try to gather as much information as you can about loans and financial aids that you are entitled to, as a single mother.

Keep yourself updated with the laws and legal framework. This helps in the management of finances in a better way, especially in cases like divorce or separation.

Associate yourself with support groups for single mothers. These groups are emerging in many cities and cater to the problems faced by single mothers.

Chapter 2: Types Of Parenting Styles

The type of approach you apply when it comes to disciplining your children may have a huge impact on their development. In addition, the parenting style can also determine the kind of relationship you will have with your child. The different parenting approaches can even have a significant impact on your child's temperament and mood well into adulthood. Research has found four types of parenting styles, which all depend on the deficiency you feel you need to fill into the child. Therefore, different parenting styles apply different approaches when it comes to discipline.

*Authoritarian parenting

In this kind of approach, you as the parents set the rules and expect the children to follow them without excuses. The kids in this case do not have a say when it comes to solving obstacles or challenges. Rather, the children are expected to follow the rules all the time. In case a child challenges any of the rules, the normal response is usually "Because I said so". The kids are usually not given any reasons for the rules and neither are they given room for negotiation. In this style, the parents tend to use punishments rather than consequences. The problem is that, while you may succeed in bringing up law-abiding children, chances are that they will grow up with self esteem problems. In some instances, the children tend to become aggressive or hostile by focusing more on channeling out their anger towards their parents rather than learning how to solve problems and make decisions.

*Authoritative parenting

With this parenting style, the parents too have established rules that the children are expected to follow to the latter. However, the difference is that there are a few exceptions to the rule. In this case, you often tell the children the reasons for a given rule and are also considerate for the child's feelings when you are setting limits. Unlike in authoritarian parenting, in this kind of parenthood you use consequences rather than punishments. Generally, the consequences are positive in order to reinforce good behaviors and the parents are more willing to use praise and reward systems. Most children raised this way tend to be successful and happy. They are often able to make good decisions and evaluate safety risks on their own. In most cases, they also grow up to be responsible adults who are comfortable expressing their own opinions.

*Permissive parenting

This type of parenting does not allow for much discipline in the children. With this parenting, the parents are very lenient and only tend to interfere with their child's behavior when there is serious trouble. In some cases there are set consequences for certain behaviors, but the parents have a tendency to think that kids will just be kids. In this case, you as a parent take on more of a friend role, rather than a parent role. While the parent may encourage the children to open to them about their problems, they do not necessarily discourage many bad behaviors. Raising your kid this way is more likely to cause some problems in their academics. They may also tend to exhibit behavioral problems because they do not so much appreciate rules and authority. Most cases report low self esteems and a lot of sadness.

*Uninvolved parenting

This kind of parenthood tends to be very neglectful. In this case, the parents do not meet the basic needs of the children and sometimes even expect the kids to raise themselves. In most of these cases, the parent usually has substance abuse problems or mental health issues. On the other hand, they could also be lacking knowledge in child development and parenting, or they feel overwhelmed by other problems in life. Uninvolved parents normally have little clues as to what their children are doing. Rules and expectations are few, if any. Children often do not receive any guidance or nurturing and they lack the necessary parental attention. Children who grow up with uninvolved parents usually have low self esteem and perform poorly in school. They also show frequent behavior problems and are often unhappy.

Determining A Discipline Strategy

Sometimes parents do not necessarily apply one parenting strategy. Sometimes they may be more authoritarian and other times they may be more authoritative. Moreover, their discipline strategies may also vary, depending on the child. When looking for a discipline strategy to employ, it is vital that you think about exactly what you want to instill in your child. Employing effective discipline strategies can help transform your kids into responsible adults who can make their own healthy decisions. However, each parent has a different role to play in a child's upbringing and in molding him or her to be a responsible adult. Fathers and mothers have different places and roles to play in bringing up children. In the next segment, we shall talk more about that.

Chapter 3: On Realism, Practicality, And Determination

RULE #4 – Live in Reality

Every child is born with a natural survival mechanism making him or her territorial. They often use the pronoun "I" and would repeatedly chant the word "mine". As your child grows from toddler to school age and on into teenage life, he/she will probably go through the selfish, territorial phase. This behavior may upset you as a parent but know that this is just part of growing up. Your child will soon outdo this phase and this is where you teach him that life has limits and he can't always have it his way. Soon enough, the child learns to accept realism and not rely on people to serve his needs.

Of course, every parent would want to give the best for their children and treat them like princes and princesses. This is but normal and healthy. But it can be dangerous. The damage comes when a single parent indulges a child to the point that he/she is always at the receiving end. The solution? Teach him that gifts, attention, and love are delightful things, but he must learn to appreciate and be grateful for them. Never make your child feel that he is entitled to receiving them.

RULE #5 – Be Practical

Children, in order to win in this life, must learn to be practical. Life is the way it is. As a sole parent, when your child is faced with a difficult situation, you may try asking this simple question – "What can you do about it?" Believe it or not, it is one of the most effective questions for situations he will be facing throughout his life. Inevitably, your child will experience pain, failure, and rejection. People will die. He will experience loss. He will not be invited to a party nor have a date in the prom. He might get into trouble. He sure will encounter different kinds of problems just like anybody else. But if he is to live a substantive life, he will decide what to do with his problems and not rely on others to solve it for him.

Do not let your children grow up to be the victim of life. This culture already has so many victims and sadly, people love them. So we unintentionally create people who are helpless, needy, and incapable. But you, as a parent, can prevent that. Teach your children that they need to take actions. Action cures, action helps. Action engages the will and it is through action that your children will realize that they, and not others, will determine their fate.

RULE # 6 – Be Determined

Children's emotions are overflowing with impulses that, if acted upon, could lead towards their destruction. Your job as a sole parent is to help them keep their emotions always in check. This requires a great deal of perseverance and you have to do it since you are playing both a father and mother to your children. You can empathize but remember that it is more important that you guide them. How you should do it? You may try taking the following advices:

See your children more realistically and objectively

As a sole parent, it cannot be overemphasize how much your children need to have an authoritative figure in their lives. Show them the right way but make sure not to do overdo things

Make them understand how to deal with inner battles. You need to train them how to assess their impulses. Are they good or bad? Are they inspiring to make your child stronger or weaker?

Help them identify their emotions, thoughts and desires. Clarify their thinking and make their choices simple. It is important that at a young age, they are trained to weed out desires that are not necessary and help them live simply.

Teach them to fight for the right reasons – each time your child faces a difficult situation in his life, tell him that you are on his side and let him know that you will defend him provided that he is on the right side.

Chapter 4: De-Gadgetizing Your Child

As I had mentioned in a previous chapter, not everything is as easy as picking up a gadget and finding a solution or a remedy to a problem. While this book not only helps you out in raising your child and helping him have a gadget free childhood, I also share with you some of the tips and tricks that have worked for me and my children. As a full-time working parent, it can be difficult to keep monitoring your child all the time. However, if we learn to prioritize our schedules in a manner where it allows us to spend some time with our children, the tips mentioned below will help you develop a wonderful bond with your child. After all, nobody would like to be remembered as a parent who was never there for their child, would they?

Shared below are some gadget-free ways of keeping your child engaged and having fun at the same time while learning how to be independent by themselves too!

1. Crafting

If you have a whole room filled with things you have never had time to get rid of, items like bottle caps, empty glass bottles, cardboard, egg cartons, Soda pop bottles etc.., all you need to do is look for inspiration in your house. The next thing you know is you will come up with some creative idea and what better way in getting your children involved in it? Visit a store with your kids, and let them pick out their favorite paint colors, gently recommend ideas to them so that they know how else they can work with the items at home. Push them to think about what they can do by repurposing stuff available at home. You will be astonished at how a child's mind works when pushed to think creatively. The good thing about craft is you do not have to spend every dollar in your bank account and you can recycle things in the house.

For e.g.: A hanging flower pot can be made with the help of empty plastic soda pop bottles.

If creativity seems to elude you, log on to the internet and visit sites which can help you with ideas as well as give you instructions on how to go about with the craft project and also provide you with information on what all you would require to complete the project.

Most stationery marts would have tools which can be used by children as well. Don't worry about the mess that's made, after all childhood is about being messy and not perfect, isn't it?

Crafting not only helps to boost the creative cells in your children, you will also be spending some fun time with your child. Look at a project which your child would love and not something where you have to do all the work. This will also give your child the opportunity to learn how to glue things together (go slow with the glue though, you wouldn't want everything being glued together in the house), how to use the scissor etc. Sounds like fun, doesn't it? You do not necessarily have to enroll your child with an art and craft class. However if you do have an older child, it will help him/her to enroll with an art and craft class since it will help in building their socializing skills and learn teamwork when they're young. It will also help inculcate values like sharing their things with others, and who knows you might just be able to help your child make real friends for life, instead of being in front of a gadget all the time.

2.HEAD OUTDOORS

As a kid myself, going hiking or just a visit to the beach with my parents was the most joyous thing ever! I would plan for the entire day. However, since most of us now live in cities and with soaring rental and hotel prices, it is difficult for families to plan a grand vacation as they find it unaffordable. But it isn't all that difficult. You will surely be able to find a small cottage or an affordable beach trailer to rent out for a weekend. Heading outdoors is becoming obsolete these days and the only exercise kids get is using their fingers on a gadget while playing on an X-box or the laptop. The easiest way to help de-gadgetize your kids is to take them to parks or when the weather permits, teach them how to ride a bike or rollerblade in the park next door.

If you do your research well, you may even be able to convince a friend or a colleague at work to let your rent out their beach house or cabin in the woods for a getaway with the kids. Some holiday resorts even have enclosed surroundings which have the illusion of being outside. So while you relax, your kids can play instead of being indoors all the time and they won't require constant supervision. Visit a place where your child has the option to go outside and play, or go for an overnight camp. Once children get used to the outdoors, you won't find them seated in front of any gadgets when you return from work.

3. Music / Reading

Reading and music are two hobbies which have been proved by research to have some fantastic benefits in kids who are exposed to them at a younger age in life. While you may love to read or listen to music or enjoy both of them, reading books to your children that are deemed appropriate for their age will result in some wonderful rewards at school and in life for your child. While you should not force your child to master an instrument only because the neighbor's kid is a maestro, encouraging your child to pick up and learn music instrument will be a fun activity for them. If your child does not show any interest in learning an instrument, do not fret. While not all of us may like to play an instrument, we all sure do share our love for music, don't we? Play the radio at home, or if you have any of your old vinyl's, music C.D's etc.., play them on your music system at home. Not only will your child learn to love the various sounds, you will surely not regret developing a good taste for music in your child.

Take your child to a library where there are plenty of options available. What you read as a child may not really interest your own child. Don't force a book or an author on your children. Let them learn to choose a book for themselves. Take them to the children section in a library, or if you prefer online shopping, then you can look up books or speak with your child's class teacher and ask for recommendations on books they feel are suitable enough for you to read to your child or books which your child can learn to read.

4. Bring out the Sous Chef in Your Child

When kids often say the words every mother detests hearing, "I'm bored." you know you are going to have to find a remedy for their boredom even though you have tons of work still not checked off your to-do list.

Try to find kid-friendly recipes online, like cupcakes or a pizza. With cupcakes, kids love to get involved and help with frosting the cupcakes and personalize the cupcakes with their favorite toppings. With pizza, kids love rolling out the dough and you won't believe it but with getting your child to make the pizza, you might just be able to sneak in some of the vegetables your child detests eating otherwise. Children feel proud when they see their creation come out of the oven. Once you allow and teach your child what tools are harmful in the kitchen and a basic training of first-aid (just in case they get a boo-boo), they are going to feel super happy and will be more than pleased to go gloating about how they make a cupcake with their mom at home. If your child's school allows it, you can even let your child participate in the school kitchen with the knowledge that they know how to handle the food and are aware of what can injure them (like a knife, fork etc..)

5. Indoor Games

Puzzles, board games, Lego etc. are some fun ways of keeping your child entertained and away for gadgets for hours on end. It also helps in tiring out their mind if they are bored and you will be able to focus on what you're doing since they might not need constant supervision with indoor games. However, do pay attention to the age group mentioned on the game box. You don't want a two year old swallowing a puzzle piece meant for a five year old.

Lego helps in boosting their creativity skills and board games help the whole family to bond together. Puzzles can keep children occupied for days, they help in boosting brain activity for your child and your child will learn to find resolutions at an early age.

6. Outdoor Games

You are probably one of the lucky few if you have space outside your house for you to set up a play area for your children. Set up a basketball hoop, allow your children to learn how to dribble a ball or kick a ball around when they are young. A little bit of sunlight can do wonders for your child's bones and health!

Or if you have even more space, get a trampoline. Not only will it be fun for your child to jump about, you can join in the fun too. Make a party of it by inviting some of your child's play school friends. It will be an excellent for you and your child to socialize and the best part is there are absolutely no gadgets involved!

7. GARDENING

Being out in the garden and getting everything from their hands, feet, knees and clothes all mucky is a child's favorite attraction. Not only is gardening fun, it makes for a lovely learning and observing experience for the children. Being inquisitive and asking all kinds of questions about the plants from what kind of plants are being grown to what do plants eat and drink etc. If you live in an apartment, you can always learn through various resources online about how to grow a terrace garden or a window garden. You can even turn this into a craft project. Get the child to paint the pots, or water the plants, and watch how your child begins to get responsible about the plant.

You know your child best, so you should be aware of what he or she likes the most. Unfortunately as technology advances, some of us including me are guilty of being glued to our laptops and phones and not paying much attention to what are children try to tell us. So whether it is clay modeling or painting, building blocks and crashing them down, try to get involved and become a part of your child's world. You might just see things much differently from his perspective. Pin up his recent art work on the kitchen board, keep his latest Play-Doh creation in the drawing room, and learn to praise him for the beautiful plants growing outside. Not only will this help build his self-esteem, he will be even more encouraged to participate in such activities in school and who knows, by encouraging your child, you might just end up helping other parents by encouraging their children too!

Chapter 5: Advice For Parenting Dyslexic Child In Classroom

Parenting dyslexic children can be frustrating. It can cause emotional failure and misconceptions. Preconceived ideas link dyslexia with a lack of motivation and intelligence. The best thing that parents can do is to be knowledgeable enough in knowing all the support and needs of their children to completely guide them to the path of success. They still have the responsibility to help their child even the teachers are there. Here are also some advices about the appropriate and correct support for dyslexic children in the room:

THE COMMUNICATION

- Never think that the teacher knows everything about dyslexia. Even if the educator undergoes training, the face to face communication between the two of you is very important. You can tell the teacher about your child's ability and the ways he/she learned easier. You can also share your child's personality and attitude so that the teacher can handle your child better. It is very important to have an everyday communication with the teacher about your child's progress. This communication will be beneficial for you as a parent because you can closely monitor your child and be alert on the signs of emotional failure or anger. Dyslexic children are more likely to suffer from emotional failure due to the stress of academic struggles. You always have to be aware on your child's progress, difficulties and problems.

THE HOMEWORK HELP

These are the things that the parents can do in helping their child with their homework:

Set the right time for doing homework. Take concern for having a break from schoolwork. Never pressure your child. Find the right time to help him do that homework.

Choose the right place for doing homework. Consider your child's preference. Choose the place wherein there are no distractions.

Be a good model in doing work habits. Your child will also be responsible if you will show him that you are responsible too. This is one of his motivations.

Help your child by coaching him in the beginning and ends of his assignment. If he encounters difficulty along the way, help him to understand.

Let your child to do his own. Discuss him all the help that you will give him and the expected things that you will account from him. Through this, you will see clearly the progress of your child.

Have some break but stay away from full interruption.

Help your child to manage a long assignment. Teach him how to break it into smaller parts.

Make sure that your child understands what to do with his homework. Take patience in explaining to him the homework expectations.

Create your own planner to organize things accordingly. This will help you to be more efficient and productive.

Reinforce your child. Ask him questions and see if he understands the lesson.

Make some suggestion but never do the homework. Help your child with it showing responsibility that he should learn.

Give more attention and time in helping him to his homework. Guide him whenever there are things that he didn't understand.

PARENTING TIPS AND ADVICES IN ASSESSING DYSLEXIC CHILD

As a parent you have the biggest responsibility in supporting your child. You have to love them unconditionally and show them your encouragement for their success. Here are some tips on parenting your child with dyslexia.

Have a lot of patience with your child.

- Your child's condition requires patience which will help you to fully understand his behavior. Every time your child commits a mistake, you should have the willingness to carry them and give them encouragement. You have to take the big picture of positive life to him.

Love your child unconditionally.

- Your love can help your child to ease the burden that he encountered because of his condition. You should make him feel that you loved him and you appreciate his existence. Never treat him as an ordinary child, but a special creation. The love that you'll show him will build a great foundation of good relationship and affection. Above all, love will be the greatest motivation for you as their parent.

Make him feel important

- No matter what your child's condition, never let him to feel unworthy. Always make him feel that he is important to you and you really care about them. Dyslexic child can be more sensitive than other child in terms of attention and care.

Never underrate them.

- As their supporter, you should believe in their capabilities and talents. You should show them that they can and they will succeed despite of their condition. Dyslexic child often feels frustrated and discouraged when it comes to potentials and abilities. They tend to think that they are inferior and weak.

Motivate them.

- Dyslexic children need more motivation and encouragement than the normal child do. They tend to be weaker and frustrated when it comes to self confidence. As their parents, you should motivate them and show them that they have the potentials and talents. Teach them them the importance of self esteem and self confidence.

Teach them discipline.

-Dyslexic child is emotional. They are more aggressive and defiant than normal child. Let your child to develop discipline knowing what the difference between right and wrong is. Teach him that punishment and scolding is sometime normal. Discipline him in a way that he could understand his mistake, not by the way that he will feel unworthy and stupid.

Develop self esteem and self confidence

- you should help your child to develop self esteem and self confidence. Through this, he will be aware to his surroundings and be more independent in taking actions considering his abilities and talents. Teach him how to be confident and efficient. He will develop productivity and high self esteem.

Support his decision

- Your child will be more confident if you will support every action that he'll take. As long as you know that it will bring him success, let it be. Don't block the road that your child wants to take. Support him and let him succeed.

Make him feel normal and comfortable

- Despite his condition, make a way on how your child will feel that he's normal. Teach him how to behave properly and how to act in every situation that he'll encounter.

Give him acknowledgement

- Praises and acknowledgement is a word of encouragement and appreciation.

When your child feels that he's appreciated, he's triggered and more willing to do better things

Chapter 6: Strategies That Work

Now that you understand what your teenagers are going through, it is time to put these strategies to work. There will be encounters, and there will be dramas. You can't say that you've raised a teenager without them. However, you can get through the drama years in less time by practicing these simple, easy to use strategies.

1. Be a good example.

As parents, the old adage, "action speaks louder" is applicable in raising teens. What they see, they do. What you do, they do. Your teens need good role models. You can help your teenagers become the best that they can be by just doing your very best in everything, every day.

2. Let your teens know that you are there for them always.

If you are having difficulty in adjusting to your teenagers, just imagine how much harder it is for them to adjust to their new status as well. Not only are they concerned with their changing looks and physiques but they have various pressures too coming from different sources. What are those pressures? The need to be responsible and to start acting like an adult can be overwhelming for them.

There is the task to establish their identities and achieve confidence and self-worth. They need supportive parents. Nagging them at this time would only add to their already stressed-filled life. They need someone who will take the time to listen to their many concerns and just be there for them. They will need you. Let them know that they are your priority.

3. Setting the limits.

It is worth the repetition – communication is a vital key to a successful parent-child relationship, even if they are teenagers. Set a time to have a heart-to-heart discussion with your teens. Let them know your rules and standards, what is allowed and what is not. On the same page, allow your teen to verbalize what is important to them, too. Hear what they have to say for themselves. When both of you have understood what is important for one another, then it is time to set limits.

Decide the rules together that are agreeable to both of you. Be specific. For example agree to the curfew time for being home. Do not just say, "be home early." Give the time. What is early for your teens may be very late for you. After you have both agreed to the time, set the disciplinary action for breaking the rules.

Try to reach an agreement on the punishment too. It could be no cellphone for a day or a cutback on the allowance. Allow room for adjustments.

The disciplinary action should not be too harsh. It should be fair for both of you, and then be consistent with what you have agreed upon. If you break the agreement, the teen will feel that you cannot be trusted. If you are not consistent, your teen will also not be consistent with the established rules and disciplines. Consistency is a must.

Check your rules once in a while to see if there are old rules that you can do without, or new rules that need to be included. Again, this is just temporary. Once the behavior is developed, you won't need the contract anymore. They will know which is appropriate or not.

4. Predicting good things for your teens.

Your words are very powerful. Your teenagers can hear them for the rest of their lives. If you keep on telling them that they are no good, then they get that idea and do what is expected of them. They will be no good, indeed. Take the time to find what is special about your teen and be generous with your praises and appreciation. If you think he is very much into basketball, then be his number one fan. If she likes to draw all those anime characters, do not try to change her subjects. Instead be supportive, and provide with art supplies.

Though teenagers seem aloof and withdrawn, try to spend time with them as much as you can. Let them know that you are available for them. Try to see the world through their eyes. Take interest in what they are doing. Always think of what is best for your teenagers. Imagine them as the successful individuals that they are destined to be. Do not think of them as difficult. Create their future with your good and kind words.

Chapter 7: Learn To Say No

This has been a subject of interest in many different households over the years. It seems to fluctuate between always say no, and always say yes. There seems to be a constant battle between the parents that feel that saying no is detrimental to a kid's self-esteem and parents that feel that saying yes is spoiling a child. The truth is that there needs to be a balance. These days, parents are all about saying yes and minimal discipline because they feel that their children's spirits will get broken.

Parents, you need to learn to say no to your child. Your child will thank you for being a stern parent later on in life. While there is a time to say yes, there is also a time to say no. It is perfectly normal to not give in to every whim of your precious angel. You are not a bad parent for saying no to a candy bar in the store or saying no to having a third snack in 2 hours, 20 minutes before dinner was done. You have every right to set boundaries in your home, and expect your toddler to follow them.

Setting Boundaries

You as the parent have to decide what is best for your child and what is okay. You also have to decide what is not okay and what you will not deal with. These are the issues that will come with punishments. You have to decide how many times to give a warning before giving a punishment as well. Children will try to push the boundaries to see how much they can get away with. It is up to you to be firm with the boundaries and to make sure that your child is not pushing too far for you.

When setting boundaries, you have to be firm. Do not keep being lenient because your child will keep breaking the rules. Everything a toddler does is cute to the parents. Not so much to the people around you though. Also, allowing your child to break the rules can give them a problem with lack of respect for authorities. This can be a big problem because if they do not respect the people in charge, it will only get worse as they get older. Set boundaries and stick to them.

If your child throws a tantrum, you should definitely stand your ground. A lot of parents will give in to their child, especially in public, because they fear they are a bad parent for letting their children cry. If you teach your child that throwing a tantrum is okay, they will do it for as long as they possibly can, and it is really hard to break that habit. Make sure to stick with your original statement no matter how much they scream. If you are in public, you may have to remove them from the situation.

Setting Boundaries with Other People

Ah, grandparents. The people who believe that they trump everyone. It is a common misconception that grandparents have a right to spoil their grandchildren, when that is not the truth. Unless they are raising the child, they do not get to blatantly disregard your rules as a parent. If you say no, that means no. They do not have the right to undermine your authority no matter if they are babysitting or you are in the room. If your child realizes that you will say no, but grandparents will say yes, then they will play that card to their advantage, making it harder for you to parent your child your way.

So, you have to set boundaries with the people that are around you. You need to let people know what you are okay with and what you are not okay with. A lot of people have trouble speaking up to family members, especially if what they are doing is not harmful to the child. However, if it is making you uncomfortable, say no. If people want to protest, remind them that they are not raising your child, you are. Many people mean well, but they just don't realize how much it undermines parental authority to do what the parent said no to.

Ignore the Unsolicited Advice

Everyone has something to say. Most of the time, there will be a lot of people who think they know better than you do, even if they do not have children. You have to learn to ignore the advice or politely decline it. Remember, these people do not know your child like you do, and a lot of people do not realize that every child is different.

One of the things you will get the most flak on is discipline. It seems like any way you would discipline your child is wrong to someone. However, the only people that matter are you and your child. As a parent, or parents, you have the right to discipline your child within the legal means. You also have the right to decide what disciplines are okay for other people watching your child to use.

When people start to tell you how to raise your child, do not get angry. Show your child how to respectfully disagree with people. Kindly remind them that every child is different and that you want to do what is best for your child. If they start to protest and try to find reasons that they know better, it is best to just say that you agree to disagree and walk away. This will show your child that arguments do not have to escalate to anger, and you will give your toddler a great lesson in compassion.

Parents have got to learn to say no. Children watch everything you do, and you want to teach them to stand up for themselves. You also do not want to let them walk all over you. You want to show your children that there are rules and that rules will be enforced. By learning to say no, you teach your toddler a plethora of valuable morals.

Chapter 8: How To End Sibling Rivalry: How To React And What To Do When Your Children Start Fighting

Infighting between children is normal and common. When you children quarrel and fight, it affects the family as a whole. Your maternal instinct is to intervene when the fighting starts because you do not want it to affect the family.

While this is maternal, you must avoid it; when the fighting starts, only step in if your children are threatening to hurt each other physically. Intervening consistently denies your children a chance to learn how to resolve their issues and in some cases, goes as far as creating other problems that may take longer to resolve.

For instance, when your children accustom to your intervention each time they argue or quarrel, they will adopt the behavior or habit of waiting on you to come be their savior, to solve their problems for them. This means that at the end of it, they will not learn how to get along or solve their problems.

By intervening all the time, you also risk the chance of escalating resentment and jealousy especially if one child feels shortchanged or as if the other child receives special treatment. This is especially so because when you intervene, you will fall into the temptation to play judge.

When you notice your children using harsh language when arguing with each other, the best thing you can do is impress upon the children that words have the ability to wound and then teach them how to express their feelings appropriately using appropriate words.

This differs from stepping in to separate arguing kids in that because you are using the present situation to teach both children how to communicate their emotions effectively, no child will feel as if the other child "gets away" with—specifically the child you rescue—with most things.

A great way to do this is to do so playfully. For instance, Otilia Mantelers, parenting instructor from Romania suggests that when children are using negative language on each other, language such as you are ugly or stupid, instead of stepping in and asking them to stop, the best thing you can do is divert the insults on yourself. For example, if one child says to the other, "you are so ugly," you can quip in and say—loudly enough for both children to hear—"I hope no one ever says I am stupid or ugly. If someone did, it would hurt so much, especially if it's someone I care about."

You can dramatize you are upset by hiding your face under a towel. Your children are likely to respond to this especially if you are feeling hurt and show them how serious you are about hiding your face and never revealing it ever again.

For a more 'systematic' approach to ending sibling rivalry, do the following:

Step 1: Avoid being a judge

When your children fight especially when they are fighting over toys or who gets to control the remote, you are likely to say something such as, "you better share or I will take X or Y away from both of you." "You are also likely to want to resolve the issue by playing mediator. For instance, you are likely to ask the children to play in turns; this has the effect of making the child that has to play with the toy second feel unwanted.

While stepping in and playing judge seems like the right move, it is not; in the real sense, all it does is foster feelings of resentment and further competition for your attention and love.

Instead of stepping in and playing the role of judge, you should validate your children's emotions as a way to show them it is OK to feel hurt or a specific way. By reflecting their feelings on them, you will help them see these emotions and feelings as just that, feelings and emotions that they can manage.

If you do this effectively, you will show your children how to look at problems and feelings from the other person's perspective, which as you can guess and imagine, has the effect of teaching your child how to handle difficult situations, emotions, and feelings in a productive, nonaggressive manner. Obviously, you and your partner have to talk the talk and walk the walk.

As an illusory example of how this would play out, assume you find one child crying and when you ask about it, the child not crying says, "I did nothing!" In such a case, playing the role of judge, you would say something such as, "You did something. If you did nothing, why is she crying? Please let your brother/sister be; stop bothering her."

On the face of it, this seems like a perfectly reasonable approach. However, upon closer analysis, you can see the connotation behind it: that one child has won. This breeds further resentment and ensures constant infighting and rivalry.

Instead of saying this, try saying something such as, "Oh. I understand that getting along with your brother/sister is not easy. Perhaps he is feeling hurt because you accidentally said or did something that hurt him/her?"

This is a very effective way to handle the situation especially because other than helping your children calm down and see how what they do and say may affect other people, it will keep you calm.

It lets your children know that not getting along is part of life especially family life.

Step 2: Help them defocus on the problem and focus on the solution

After spending a fair amount of time helping your children reflect on their emotions and feelings, the next immediate step is to help them—not you—to solve the conflict by suggesting—or asking them to suggest—solutions on how they can get along.

For instance, once you have used the above step to reflect their feelings in a positive way that helps them understand each other's emotions, you can ask something such as, "I know that wanting to watch something different from what your sister wants to watch is difficult. Can you think of something you would both enjoy watching?"

The idea is to get the children thinking about solutions to the problem instead of focusing so much on what is wrong about each other. If your children are not ready to come up with a solution, try the reflection technique again, casually name the problem, and then offer some neutral solutions.

For instance, if your kids are fighting over the remote, you can say, "Only one remote and one TV; I understand why it is difficult to agree on what to watch. Do you want to hear what some other children did in the same situation? They chose to watch something they both enjoy and when they could not find something, decided to watch the TV in turns of 5 minutes."

This is the most effective to help your children handle conflict because in addition to helping the kids handle in-the-moment conflict, it also equips them with the skills they need to handle conflicts in interpersonal relationships as they grow and mature.

The process is slow—parenting is a slow process; however, be patient with them and yourself especially because although they are unlikely to come up with the answers in the moment, you will build in them the mindset of focusing on the solution instead of the problem. It also encourages cooperation, one of the most important elements you can teach your children.

Step 3: Avoid Labeling–especially negative labeling

As parents, we normally fall into the habit of placing our children in negative roles. For instance, we—and other children—can label a child a crybaby and other negative labels such as the show off.

Avoid doing this and encourage your children to avoid too because it will only worsen the rivalry especially because the labelled child will feel unloved. In most cases, children adopt this behavior by listening to how we handle our children. For instance, if you say something such as "stop being a cry baby" to one child, the other child is likely to adopt this negative habit.

Keep yourself from adopting such behavior because in addition to other children adopting the same, the entire family is likely to do the same too with the effect being that the labelled child will also start accepting the negative label as an identity.

Always keep in mind that your children adopt the label you give them. If the label you give your children is negative, your children will think it to be true, which will have a negative effect on that child's self-image and not to mention how your other children view the labelled child, which will only fuel the resentment, teasing, and arguments between your children.

Avoid negative labeling your children and if you have done so in the past, work on eliminating the same. Instead of focusing on your child's negative behavior, focus on his or her positive behavior and be communicative about this. It will help your children see each other in positive light, which will have the effect of reducing negative fights because it will foster a positive mentality.

To do this, find times when your children are acting right and point it when all the other children are around. While finding these times can be challenging, it will help reduce rivalry and help your kids get along better.

Step 4: Use pat phrases

Keeping the peace in the family is one of your most important roles. Pat phrases are one-line statements that allow you to communicate the importance of family peace and getting along. Because children hate long conversations and lectures, using one-line pat phrases is something they are likely to appreciate a lot.

Examples of pat phrases you can use when your kids are fighting and quarreling with each other include:

"We live in a family built on support and understanding."

"Teasing is hurtful."

"You have the capacity to be kind and understanding; choose to use it."

Use these one-liners as guidelines upon which you create your very own one-line pat phrases that help you keep the peace.

Chapter 9: Learn To Let Go

Once your child starts going to school, you are no longer the most important person in his/her life anymore. Shocking? Yes, I know this would come as a shock to you but that is the bitter truth. You must understand this.

Your love as a parent should be willing to let them go. They should be able to face life, fall, fail and allow them to get back up. This is the only way they can succeed. As funny as it sounds, there is no key to success. There has never been any key to success. You fall, you rise up. Such is life. And that is the path to success. When you do this, you are preparing them for adulthood.

Most parents want so much for their children. So much that the love can be blinding. That is when you hear statements like; I just want to give my child what I never had. We shouldn't compare our lives at a young age with theirs. Virtually everything is different. We should teach our children happiness in little and plenty. The first principle in this book still remains the most significant rule in parenting. Teach yourself to live an amazing life of success and your children would learn from you. Teach by doing not saying.

Being over protective would ruin the life of your child. It wouldn't give them the space needed to blossom. You should love your children, yes but make sure you give them that freedom to learn from their actions and inactions. Allow them to take responsibility.

Funny enough, an over protective parent is always like a thorn in the flesh of a child. Especially when that child has such independent lifestyle and enjoys it. Mom! I'll be fine.

Letting go is something that can be very hard to do. Your child is a big part of you. That bond is so strong. However, there comes a time that you'll need to let go. Not because you don't love them anymore but because you really love and you want them to have the best.

Today, parents battle the minefields of mobile phones, internet and social media with children. There was a time when you could walk down the street, talk to people, when you could drink free water from the fountains scattered along the street. Everything was not so mobile or digital like we have it now. Take a vacation and tell your children to come without their phones allow cameras. Walk down the street with your child and talk to random people. Go to a coffee shop and talk. Get them doing things which feel weird and make it fun. Provide rewards at the end of the day. Refuse to eat meat one day of the week or refuse a meal. Get the money you should have spent on meat or on food for that day and give it to those in need. Let that kind nature grow in them.

Don't just learn to let go, learn to do so at the right time. When you delay, you hinder maturity and adulthood. Letting go should start as early as possible so that when you are needed to make that giant step you wouldn't face any attachment problem. Some parents maybe over protective without them knowing. Let me clue you in. When you statements like; Mom! I'll be fine becomes something repeated by your daughter or son, then you know that you are the overprotective type.

The world is changing. As the world keeps changing you should also change your skills as a parent.

Chapter 10: Safe And Fun Outdoor Activities For Kids During Summer

Kids love the summer. It is when they can go out and enjoy the sun for long periods of time. Camping trips and family excursions are also being held during summer vacations. Here are activities the whole family will enjoy especially the kids during summer!

Blowing Bubbles

Kids especially love blowing bubbles. Find or buy some bubble wands. Then mix some bar soap in the water. Mix vigorously until there are bubbles everywhere. Dip the bubble wand onto the mixed solution. (Beware some soaps are not child-friendly and can get your kid's eyes teary once in contact with the soap). Blow the bubble wand and let the kids play with the bubbles. This can keep the kids busy for hours.

Water Play

Kids love to play with and on the water. They love to get wet and will be running all around the place. Prepare a garden pool (made of rubber or inflatable). Fill it with water till it's half-filled. Adorn the pool water with some rubberized ducks or rose petals. Children will definitely love to stay submerged in the pool water for longer periods of time. It is more fun and they can stay longer if they have their friends with them swimming and playing with them as well. (Beware; do not let them play with water for too long though. It is not good for their lungs. Make sure that you apply some baby oil onto their back and chest before they swim in the pool).

Gardening

Kids are not afraid to get dirty. They don't have any fear of worms, butterflies, etc. To keep them busy and safe, let them play with soil. Make sure it is garden soil/loam soil. Also make sure that before they touch the soil, their fingernails are not long so that dirt won't get into their nails. Give them a pot with soil and some grass. Have them uproot the grass first then let the kids select from the variety of plants available. Surely, they would choose the colourful ones and these can keep the child preoccupied with that activity and wouldn't want to be distracted.

Play Caterpillar Hopscotch

Draw a large chalk circle 2 or 3 feet across with feet and antennae then add 10 or 20 more circles to create a jumbo caterpillar. Challenge the kid to run or jump from one circle to the next. It will be more exciting if it's coupled with beautiful music that will serve as a stop watch. Once the music plays, the kids can hop or run around, and once it stops, the kids should stop right away as well whatever they are doing. They should not move till the music plays again. Colors can also be added on each circle for variety and the kids can hop from red to blue to green. That will give a sense of difficulty and challenge that will make it more fun for the kids.

Arrow Pointer

It's time to play a more exciting game in the backyard. Try to hide some clues anywhere like on the tree leaves, tree trunks, under a rock or anywhere in the soil. Make or draw a large arrow pointing to different directions and let the kids go to where they deem the clues are hidden. Make sure that there are corresponding prizes for this kind of activity. Rewards are a motivational tool for kids to accomplish what you want them to accomplish.

Mini Car Wash

Since youngsters love water-related activities, it is also recommended for kids to have a mini carwash in the garden. First, fill a plastic pail with water until half-full. Pour a dishwashing soap or shampoo and mix well until it is bubbly. Get a sponge and have the kids wash their toy cars and bikes. Clean it thoroughly and rinse properly with a water hose. Then, dry it and parade it in the garden.

Camping

Although kids cannot set-up a tent on their own yet, (unless they are 11 years and up) parents can still help them in setting up their tents. Once the tents are done, let the kids run around the yard and pick up some sticks or twigs for a bonfire. Just instruct them to gather as many twigs as they can and you'd be surprised that they are really enjoying this really fun activity.

Building Sand Castles on the Beach

For outing, some parents would like to have some quality time together. This can be made possible if kids will be given an exciting activity as building sand castles. They will need a plastic pail with a handle, a shovel and creativity!

Create an Obstacle Course

Let your child explore his physical strength and endurance by completing an obstacle course. Arrange some hurdles by making use of some chairs and old car tires for the obstacle course. Let your kids jump over the chair (not too high) and then run over the 4 sets of old car tires. Then Hang some sturdy cloth or rope to a low tree branch (make sure the branch is sturdy as well) and let the kids grope the rope and hang in there for like 5 seconds then go back to base.

Hide and Seek

Where can hide and seek be better played other than outdoors? Children can climb trees, hide inside the bushes or behind a rock or a tree trunk...It will be more fun and kids will definitely have more space to hide.

Blind-folded Drawing

Things needed are a chalk/marker and a board (black board/white board). Blind-fold a kid and let him go to the board. Now, draw a circle on the board and guide the kid's hand towards the center of the circle. Now have the kids draw the face on the circle...eyes, nose, mouth, ears, eyebrows and hair. It is really funny and it's guaranteed the kids won't be able to get over it at once till they laugh their hearts out once they see how the blind-folded kid drew the face...

Chapter 11: Importance Of A Clean, Safe Home Life

Children deserve to live in an environment that promotes safety and health. There are many dangers around the average home that many parents are not aware of. We will discuss some of the common dangers and how to avoid them. We will also discuss the importance of a decluttered and clean home environment.

We have all seen toys that help children by teaching them to put a square peg into a square hole and a round peg into a round hole. The reason those toys are so popular with small children is because small children love to stick objects into places. (Any parent who has ever recovered a slice of pizza from a VHS or DVD slot know this) However, this same scenario holds true with things like electrical outlets. Young children love to do two main things: they love to imitate you and they love to play pretend. If your young child sees you plug in your television, hairdryer, or phone charger to a wall outlet, he is going to want to play pretend and imitate that same move by plugging in a fork or a car key. Any retail store will have the inexpensive outlet plugs that will prevent this from happening.

Most homes have cleaners, as well as other dangerous chemicals, in them. The average person has these chemicals stored under the sink in the kitchen or in the bathrooms. Even if you are one of those parents who purchase all-natural cleaners, many of them are still harmful if swallowed or absorbed in large quantities. We need chemicals to properly maintain our homes. Things like drain openers, paint thinners, and pest control chemicals are common for household maintenance. These chemicals can be harmful, even fatal, for children. To ensure your child's safety, all dangerous chemicals should be stored in a locked cabinet or out of your child's reach.

People have different reasons for owning guns. Some people collect guns. Some people use guns for hunting. Some people choose to have guns in their home for protection and security. No matter what your reason for having a gun in your home, guns are dangerous in the wrong hands. When you have children in the house, all guns should be unloaded, locked with a trigger lock, and stored in a locked area or in an area out of your child's reach. Most local law enforcement agencies will provide you with locking devices for your guns at no charge to you.

Young children should never be allowed to have or play with knives, sharp scissors, or other sharp objects. These items should be placed and kept in an area that your child would never be able to reach. However, keeping these items stored out of your child's reach is only part of the solution. These are the types of items that many adults use regularly around the home. When you are cooking it is not uncommon to have one or two knives resting on your countertop in the kitchen area. When you are doing certain crafts or decorating it may be common to have a pair of sharp scissors laying nearby. Just remember to not have any of them within reach of your small children.

Most accidents involving children happen at home. One reason is because home is where children spend most of their time. Another reason is because, unlike a traditional daycare or classroom, your home is not set up to be completely child proofed and designed to only house children.

One of the most common child injuries reported by emergency room doctors is sprains and broken bones caused by a slip and fall. One issue is so simple it should not need much discussion. That is simple spills around the house. Your child is going to spill things. You are going to spill things. The only solution to this hazard is to clean up any spill as soon as it happens or as soon as you notice the spill.

If you have a small child in your home you may have realized that you can spend their entire nap period picking up every toy, every stuffed animal, every game and game piece, and every color crayon and placed them all neatly in the toy box and on the assigned shelves, only to have it all undone within an hour of their waking up.

One solution is to restrict your child's play area to their bedroom or to designate a specific corner in your living area where your child can play. If you do this, you need to set consequences (loss of the toy) if you find a toy outside of the designated area. Another solution is one I have found to be the most effective. Separate your children's toys as you see fit. I personally have a box containing farm animals, a box containing Disney characters, a box containing kitchen play sets, etc. All the boxes should be placed on a shelf that is not accessible to the child. Only allow the child to play with one or two of the boxes at a time and do not bring out other boxes until your child has picked up all the first two boxes of toys to be stored away.

Let's face facts. Children are not always the only mess-makers in the home. Some people are just comfortable with clutter. Some clutter may make your home feel "lived in", however, too much clutter can be dangerous.

Young children love to climb. It is in their nature. From the time they start pulling up on your furniture and learning to take their first step, they continue pulling on things and climbing higher when possible. If your home is cluttered and you have things stacked up in piles, your child will soon be trying to climb your clutter mountains. Make sure that you do not have heavy objects stacked in areas where your child could pull them over and be harmed. Keep all dining chairs pushed under the table to reduce a climbing accident there.

Many homes have unfinished repair jobs in one room or another. If you live in an area where there has been natural disasters and your home received damage, the repairs often take months to complete. Some homes are older and simply have ongoing maintenance issues. Some homes have owners who are regularly working on home improvements, expansions, and remodeling. Either way, any home with unfinished repair jobs can harbor dangers to young children.

The typical dangers from unfinished repair jobs are the tools, power tools, hardware, and items such as paint, paint thinner, and insulation that can harm children. Be sure to keep any of these items stored away when not in use or restrict your younger children from entering the areas being repaired. Also, repair jobs often leave raw electrical wires exposed. Exposed wires can cause severe electrical burns and even death. There is also the danger of electrical fires. We discuss fire safety later in the book.

Another household item that has caused numerous visits to medical professionals is uncovered lightbulbs. This is usually in the form of a lamp that has no shade covering the lightbulb. A traditional lamp shade is designed to disperse the light from the lightbulb and to tone down the brightness to a more comfortable inside light source. Removing the shade or using a lamp that has no shade may brighten up a room with harsh lighting but it has been known to attract the attention of young children who received severe burns from the bulbs.

Another danger in many homes are OTC and prescription medications. Something like one in four adults are on at least one prescription drug in America. That is an astounding number. The most common prescribed drug in people's homes are opioid drugs such as hydrocodone. The most common OTC medication in people's homes are Tylenol products. One accidental dose of some opioids can be fatal to children. One accidental high doseage of Tylenol products can cause sever liver damage and possible liver failure.

If you have children of any age in your home you should have any and all OTC and prescribed medications locked away. These are chemicals and can be deadly to children in small doses. Leaving medications sitting around on countertops or on bedside tables is an invitation to disaster.

Checklist for Basic Home Fire Safety:

For smokers, use large, deep ashtrays. Never leave burning cigarettes unattended. Never smoke in bed.

Never leave candles unattended.

Never run electrical cords under rugs.

Replace or toss any item that has a frayed electrical cord.

Never place objects, especially heavy objects, on a bed when using an electric blanket.

Place carbon monoxide alarms near all bedrooms.

Do not overload electrical outlets.

Unplug all electrical appliances when not in use, when possible.

Keep all items at least three feet away from any space heater when in use.

Install ceiling-mounted smoke alarms at least four inches away from walls.

Test all smoke alarms and carbon monoxide alarms once a month and replace the batteries twice per year.

Vacuum all smoke and carbon monoxide alarms when replacing the batteries.

Never leave anything on the stove unattended.

Keep the cooking areas clear of items that can burn.

Avoid wearing loos-fitting clothing when cooking.

Have your heating system serviced before cold weather begins.

Have heating devices with automatic shut-off.

Be sure to clean the lint-trap of your dryer before each use.

Do not leave the dryer or any appliance running while you are asleep or away from home.

Checklist for Basic Yard and Park Safety:

Never leave your child unattended in your yard or at the park.

Do not allow your child to run and play with sharp or heavy objects.

Make sure all doors are closed and locked

Chapter 12: When Family Problems Come

There will never be a perfect marriage, nor a perfect family. Every household would go through certain problems and hatches along the way. Either a simple family problem like sickness in the household, disobedient kids, and little misunderstandings between the parent and the child, or a big problem like financial crisis, separation/divorce, and even death. There are lot of problems really, but these are the most common ones that a typical family goes through.

Again, balancing work and your personal life as a parent is a hard and enduring task and so sometimes, you fall off the right track because of several reasons combined. Nobody is perfect, even parents, and that is why little family problems come up here and there. However, it does not mean that you are a bad and neglectful parent to say the least. How you deal with the problems that your household will go through will determine how good or bad of a parent you are.

Good parenting is when you face a family crisis and/or problem head strong. May it be little or big, simple or complicated, you need to acknowledge and address it properly. Do not try and deny the problems you are facing as a parent or as a family because usually, small problems turn into big ones because they were left unattended. You do not want this from happening in your homes and good parents would not allow it.

Small and tiny household problems are easy to solve once you know the cause behind it. Always look at where the problem came from and start solving it from there rather than solving the outcomes first that came from a root problem. This way, you address the main and core problem first and solving the rest will be easily already.

An example of a minor problem that is most commonly experienced by every household is sickness in the home. A parent will really experience getting sick even once in his or her lifetime due to exhaustion from work. A child, on the other hand, will get sick due to exhaustion from school or accumulating a viral sickness since kids have lower tolerance from their immune system.

When faced with situations like this, it is important that you do not let the sickness get any worse before doing measures to treat them. As a parent, it is your responsibility to always keep everyone in the family fit and healthy. There is this saying that prevention is better than cure, and a good parent should take note of this. Do not wait for someone in the family to get sick. Make sure everyone is healthy starting from the food your family needs to eat to the vitamins your family needs to take. Being busy is not an excuse to undermine this simply yet important task.

For busy parents a good tip is to pre-cook meals and freeze them during weekends or days off from work so you would have homemade dinners and not store bought during the weekdays. You could also prepare simply snacks like that are healthy for your kids to eat in school. This way both you and your kids can eat something nutritious and not just fast-food products.

However, if and so a family member gets sick, do not hesitate to go to a doctor for a check-up. This will be the safest and most immediate thing you can do in order to avoid the spread of sickness to other family members in the household.

Another common problem that a family faces is disobedient kids. Sometimes, your child refuses to obey your rules and commands, especially when they are in their adolescent years. When this happens, do not forget to show authority over them. Show them who the boss is and win the power battle. However, you also have to look at the main cause of the disobedience of your child. Talk to him or her and hear their side. This will give them a sense of reassurance that their mom or dad listens, and thus, respecting you more.

With respect comes obedience and that will automatically solve your problem.

In the household, there are often misunderstandings between both parents toward each other, within siblings, and even towards a parent and his or her child. This is also a common problem that every family encounters. When this happens, the only thing to do in order to solve it is through talking and communicating. Good parents do not just argue without reasonable grounds. You have to choose your battles, especially those with your husband or wife and with your kids. Always put in mind the question "Is it worth putting your relationship on the line because of this argument?"

In some situations wherein there is already an existing tension and misunderstanding about a certain issue or topic, what you can do to solve this and avoid this in the long run is to sit down as a family and talk about it. Do not be afraid to open up to your kids because this will help both parties to understand each of your situations better to come up with mutual understandings. It is some kind of a family therapy wherein you meet as a family and talk about issues and problems in order to solve it from its root cause.

Big and immense problems are harder and more complicated to solve and address. Some of these problems cannot even be resolved which can put the family in a load of stress that can either make or break them. However, in situations like this, it is always best to try and access the problem before resulting to drastic measures that could put more stress and emotional damage to your kids.

An example of a major problem that a family can face is separation or divorce.

This is a very big issue for the family because not only does it involve both parents splitting up, but the children are also detaching themselves from the family that they have known and grew up into their whole lives. Imagine the psychological implications of your split which will affect not only you, as an individual and as a parent, but your kids as well.

There are a lot of situations and reasons that could lead a couple into separation and/or divorce. It could be because of financial problems, lack of communication, lack of trust, jealousy, infidelity, insecurity, vices and other addictions or several other reasons. However, what most couples fail to understand is that separation and/or divorce almost never happens all of a sudden. A problem or a combination of problems constantly build up over weeks and months or even years of not addressing and talking about it. When it reaches a breaking point, the whole foundation of the marriage comes crashing along with all of those problems.

As a parent, you do not want that to happen to your marriage and your family. You do not want your kids to go through that painful stage of fights and arguments and constant battles. There would be consequences for this that your child will carry as he or she grows up until the time he or she decides to marry. It will be imprinted in their minds how awful and hurting the whole process was. Not to mention custody battles, court hearing and visiting rights. Your child deserves better than this, so as your family that you have cared for, for a long time.

No matter how you put it, separation and divorce is a painful scar. However, it can be avoided by constant communication between couples. Observe and look for signs of the above-mentioned reasons that could sprout doubt in your relationship. Do not hesitate to talk to a professional if the need arises because this will help you maintain a good balance between parenting and maintaining your married life at bay.

Another major problem that a family can go through, which might be the hardest, is death. There will come a time where a family member will be taken away from you and this will probably be the saddest and hardest problem to surpass. It may be a parent or a child, but no matter who is it and when will it happen, the pain that the family will endure would not be lessened.

Now as a parent, it is your responsibility to be the rock and stronghold of the family. You cannot lessen the pain that each member might feel but it is better to stand firm for them. Show them the positive side to their darkest hour. Grieve and comfort each other in a way that would bring your family closer and not drift apart. Go to grief counselling if it will help your kids more. Do whatever it takes to bring back your normal routine. And by any consolation, pray together and trust that God has better plans for the family.

Whether you prepare for it or not, your family will go through several problems and mishaps along the way. What distinguishes you from being a good parent is how you handle them. Always remember to approach it head on and address it as early as possible to avoid further break-outs.

Chapter 13: How To Handle Temper Tantrums

Children express their frustrations with various challenges through tantrums. Maybe your toddler is having difficulties in completing a specific task? Perhaps they don't have the right words to express what they feel? Frustrations play a major role in triggering anger that leads to tantrums. Let's look at the various ways to handle tantrums in children.

I. Take the right steps to prevent the tantrums.

Schedule some frequent playtime with your little one. Allow them to choose the activity and make sure the child gets complete attention from you. Sharing a positive experience will offer your child an excellent foundation to calm herself down whenever they get upset. Check out the opportunities that will acknowledge her excellent performance. When a child receives favorable attention for the desired performance, they'll then form a habit of doing the same.

You can also create good tactics to deal with the frustrations immediately, like taking a deep breath. It's also essential to fess up after being angry over something. That's because your child needs to know it's OK to make mistakes once in a while. Make sure you know the things that lead to the tantrum and plan well. If the child gets frustrated when they're hungry, try to carry some healthy snacks. If the child starts grumbling when tired, try to make sleep time a priority.

II. Speak whenever the child yells

Your toddler will match the tone of your voice since they want to get your attention. Bear in mind, they're feeling angry and sad might assist you to remain calm. Whenever they lose control at a public spot such as the movies, take the child outside. Allow them to sit on the bench or in the car as they settle down. For most children, having such choices will help, mainly if lack of control causes the outburst.

During a post-tantrum, try to follow through with the first demand that caused the outburst. If the child became frustrated because you asked them to collect the toy, they could still get it when they're calm. If the child started screaming because you didn't allow them to have a cookie, then give the cookie once they stop crying. When the child follows through and collects the toy, applaud the child. That's because it's a positive habit you'll want to instill in them.

III. Know why your toddler reacts strongly.

While your child can use words to express what they want, that doesn't imply that the tantrums have ended. They're still learning ways to handle emotions, and a slight disagreement will make them frustrated and sad. Since your toddler values their growing independence, requiring your help might be frustrating. They might break down when trying to complete a challenging task such as tying shoelaces, and finds out they cannot do the job alone. Even though tantrums tend to start with anger, they're always deep-rooted in sadness. Children might get lost in how unjust and huge a situation becomes, so they struggle with how to do the task successfully.

Attempt this one tactic for tantrums for children below two and a half years. In most cases, children within this age bracket have 50 words in their vocabulary and can't link over two words together at a time. The child's communication is limited, but they have countless thoughts, needs, and wishes that must be met. When you fail to understand what they want, they tend to freak out to express their sadness and frustration. The remedy for this is to teach the children how to sign some words like milk, food, and tired. Empathizing with your child is another method to deal with outbursts. It assists in curbing the tantrums.

IV. Give your child some space and create a diversion.

In most cases, a child is supposed to get rid of the anger. So, just let them do it. This method will help your child know how to vent in a nondestructive manner. They'll have a chance to release their feelings, get themselves together, and recover self-control. Your child will engage in a yelling contest or fight with you. This approach can work in tandem with ignoring it a bit.

This entails a definite mental switcheroo. Try to get your child engaged and interested in other things to make her forget about the bad experience. Make sure your backpack or purse has all kinds of distractions such as toys, comic books, and yummy snacks. Once your child starts throwing tantrums, get the distraction out to catch your child's attention.

Note that a distraction can assist you in warding off a huge outburst before it occurs, provided you catch it in time. If you realize that your child is about to yell at the store since you don't want to buy them what they want, try to switch gears and enthusiastically say something such as "Hey, do we need some bread. Do you want to assist me in getting a kind?" children tend to have a short attention duration, and this makes it easy to divert their attention. When doing this, make sure you sound psyched as it will make your child know it's real. They'll tend to forget about what made them feel sad and focus on the next better thing.

V. Offer a big and tight hug.

This might feel the hardest thing to do when your toddler is acting up, but it'll assist them to calm down. This should be a big tight hug and never say anything when doing it. Hugs will make your child feel secure and allow them to understand you care about them, even though you don't support the tantrum habits. In most cases, a child needs a safe place to release one's emotions.

VI. Give them food or suggest some R&R

Getting tired and being hungry is the leading cause of tantrums in children. Since the child is on the brink emotionally, an outburst will quickly occur. Most parents keep wondering why their child has meltdowns that occur during the same time every day. For instance, many toddlers tantrum before lunch and in the evening, which is never a coincidence. If you're experiencing this, make sure you feed your child well and give them enough water. After that, let her veg, whether it involves taking her to bed or letting her watch TV.

VII. Give the child incentive to behave.

Some situations tend to be trying for children. They can encompass sitting for long hours in a restaurant when eating or staying calm in church. Irrespective of the scenario, the tactic is about noticing when you're asking for too much from your child. Also, remember to give them the incentive for the good work done. While heading to the restaurant, for instance, tell her," Maya, mom wants you to sit and take your dinner nicely. I know you'll do that! And if you behave well, you'll play your video games when we get home. This type of bribery is perfectly provided. It's done as per your terms and before time and not under pressure in the middle of a tantrum. In case she begins to lose her temper, remind her about your promise. It's great how it'll suddenly guide her back into shape.

VIII. Laugh it off.

As a parent, you fear public tantrums for various reasons. You're probably afraid other people will brand you a bad parent, or that you're raising an out of control child. However, that might lure you into making some choice that will result in deep fits. Children are always smart, even the little ones. If you get stressed and angry, allow them to find the best way to end the outburst before many people begin staring, they'll learn on her own. The best thing is to suck it up, put on a smile, and pretend that everything is OK.

IX. Get out of that place

Getting your little one away from the place of a tantrum will subdue the outburst. Additionally, it's an ideal strategy when you're in public places. When your child starts yelling over candy bars or a toy they want, take the child to a different place within the supermarket or even outside until they stop crying. Shifting the place will likely change the behavior.

Chapter 14: Advice From Parents

1 'If possible, spare at least an hour a day for yourself: enjoy a face mask, a book, favorite hobby. In general, you need to take care of yourself; this will calm you down and return the joy.'

2 'One friend of mine, instead of shouting or swearing, says in a singsong voice: 'Oh what-aa-at do I see?' Without increasing his voice at all. He both expresses his feelings and doesn't make noise.'

3 If you cannot help calling the child with bad words, at least, don't say anything like 'fool' or 'dummy.' For example, tell him: 'You are sausage.' Also, instead of raising your voice at the child, you can make faces or play the pantomime. You can growl or grunt while in anger... In general, the best remedy for violence is humor!

4 It's all about the mom's health. A happy mother is a good mother. Sometimes she needs to speak severely. But the main thing is to make the child know that his mom loves him. Every night before going to bed, tell him this, caress, hug and kiss him. Then, even a strict situation will be taken as a separate case, in which mom shows strictness, and that is not the general trend. This is what I do.

5 I observed another mother when, being angry at a naughty daughter, instead of shouting, she gave her an exaggeratedly

ferocious look and chased her with the words, 'Beware, I'll catch you!', the daughter ran, with the mother running behind her. An awkward situation was turned into a game in a twinkle of an eye.

6 Try growling or howling instead of shouting at the child... This will prevent you from telling offensive words to the kid, words for which you will be sorry when you calm down.

7 It would help if you showed children of all ages, even infants, about your mood and condition. It would help if you always said that you're in a bad mood or tired. They will understand everything, and the fact that this mood or condition may be followed by a scream or something similar will be admitted much more accessible by your child.

8 You can shout, but your voice should have no faint notes of hatred and aggression, this is what frightens the child and hurts him deeply...

9 If you rail at the child, it is essential to talk about his bad behavior, evil deed, but not to go personal, not to humiliate... You should always remember and stress this in a conversation with your child: he is good as he is, he only misbehaved, ugly, etc. Do not apply labels!

10 Most adults know how to pull themselves together when they need to. For example, you control yourself in a conversation with your boss, because you're afraid of losing your jobs... For regret, we don't treat our children with such care. Perhaps, we'll learn to resolve conflicts with the children constructively due to fear of losing a child's respect and

love for us, fear to destroy the relations of trust between us with one evil word...

Chapter 15: Labor And Birth

Nature seems to have tied love to the survival of a woman in labor. The huge amount of oxytocin flowing through her bloodstream produces the contractions that gradually push the baby down the birth canal and out into the world. At the same time, oxytocin reduces her pain and keeps her calm. This oxytocin causes her to crave a quiet, safe place to give birth, and it increases the bond she already feels for her baby.

In ancient times, all of this — the instinct for safety and quiet, the calm, the attachment of mother to baby — increased the likelihood that the mother would be able to deliver her baby and keep it from harm. Today, she doesn't need to find a nice cave in order to be safe during her labor, but she still craves quiet and stillness.

The extra oxytocin flowing through her bloodstream and the baby's, by way of the placenta, may activate the oxytocin receptors in the baby's brain. Some infant psychology experts believe that the birth experience actually "sets" the sensitivity of the baby's oxytocin receptors. In any case, it's well documented that the oxytocin receptors in the brain tend to respond to oxytocin by synching up and releasing even more, in a positive feedback loop.

When the receptors in the developing baby's brain come into contact with enough oxytocin, they get set to a point where it's easy for them to take up oxytocin later in life.

In order to develop a healthy oxytocin response, it may be that a baby's brain needs the right amount of oxytocin during birth and for a short period after it. Just enough, and her brain's oxytocin receptors begin to bloom, opening up to be able to translate this neurochemical into feelings of love and intimacy.

Hurried in the hospital

One especially critical period may begin as the baby enters the birth canal; some midwives believe that the birth experience itself sets the reactivity of the limbic system, the part of the brain that produces and controls emotions and the body's involuntary processes. According to this theory, the tone of a baby's first moments out of the womb creates an emotional set point, just as you'd set a thermostat. A frightening experience sets the baby's amygdala to high alert, limiting how much the baby can calm down. A soothing birth experience, they believe, will enable the baby to experience deep relaxation and peace, while his rages and fears won't be as intense.

Today, most women in the United States give birth in the "safe" environment of a hospital. But modern birthing practices can hinder the natural oxytocin response and immediate attachment of mother to baby.

Although she may know — with the thinking part of her brain — that the strangers rushing around are there to help her, the laboring woman's amygdala, the fear center, may become very stressed during the medical procedures taking place in the brightly lit and rather unwelcoming hospital environment. This stress may increase her levels of cortisol and adrenaline, the fear chemicals, instead of increasing oxytocin.

In addition, it's routine for hospitals to administer artificial oxytocin in order to make sure that labor proceeds according to a predetermined schedule. Often, this continuous dose of oxytocin causes contractions that are very strong and painful, and that come without respite.

This pain and fear overwhelm the laboring woman's natural oxytocin response, keeping her from enjoying the final moments before the baby is born. Her pain and fear may be transmitted to the baby, making his first experience of the world frightening instead of comforting.

Hormonal imprinting

Our ability to enjoy the bonding effects of oxytocin — the number, distribution and sensitivity of oxytocin-producing cells and their receptors — may be shaped during labor and birth by a process that Gyorgy

Csaba, a biologist at Semmelweis University in Hungary, calls hormonal imprinting.

Csaba thinks there's a critical period when developing receptor cells first encounter the hormones they bind with. How strong the hormonal bath is determines how sensitive that receptor is and sets its binding capacity for the cell's life.

Sue Carter is director of the Brain Body Center at the University of Illinois, and one of the leading researchers on oxytocin's role in bonding. Her studies of animals suggest that the oxytocin system can be "tuned" in early development, permanently changing its sensitivity to hormonal fluctuations. She writes that exposing newborn nervous systems to pitocin may "reprogram the nervous system, altering thresholds for sociality, emotionality and aggression." Moreover, she thinks that the body's future production of oxytocin is especially vulnerable to postnatal experience.

If the baby was pulled out by forceps or vacuum extraction, his body's first experience is pain and terror. This hormonal imprint can have lifelong consequences on behavior and on the ability to love.

Whether it's trauma before the child is born or following birth, it can be stored as the child's earliest memory, called the state level. This memory can be actively triggered throughout the rest of a person's life.

Early traumas for infants before birth or just following birth can set the child up to be much more sensitive to stress, fear, and stimulation than other children. These experiences can create difficulty for the child in active settings such as family time, shopping or school.

Hospital vs. midwife

Doctors save lives, and hospital birth may be the best option for you.

At the same time, there's intense societal pressure to have the modern version of a traditional birth: Lying in a hospital bed with a fetal monitor attached, oxytocin dripping through an IV, and an epidural to take away all feeling below the waist. Even the medical profession has begun to realize that these procedures may not be necessary in all cases or even improve outcomes.

Natural childbirth has been positioned as an experience of overwhelming pain and trauma. But many women find that it's actually less painful than a medical birth. Ancient ways, such as letting the laboring woman move around, letting gravity help push the baby down the birth canal when she's upright or floating in water to relieve pressure and pain turn out to work just as well for modern women.

TV personality Ricki Lake has become an advocate of natural birth with her documentary, "The Business of Being Born." It makes a strong case for choosing the least medical interventions possible when giving birth.

If you have the resources, consider alternatives including birth at home with a licensed midwife or using a hospital birthing center. Birthing centers have sprung up all over the nation. They feature private rooms with residential furniture and the option of having your birth attended by your own obstetrician or midwife.

Even if your doctor recommends that you give birth in the standard hospital setting, you can still begin Oxytocin Parenting as soon as you deliver the baby. According to Marshall Klaus, M.D. one of the co-authors of the book Bonding, wonderful things can happen between mother and baby in the first hour of life. Bonding recommends that, as soon as possible, the parents have a period of at least one hour alone with the baby.

During this time, babies seem especially open to the first connection with their parents. They typically look around and, if placed on the mother's stomach, will crawl up to the breast. It's the beginning of a sensory dialog between the baby and his parents that is the first step to intimacy.

You have the opportunity to get a great start on your Oxytocin Parenting during labor and birth. If it makes sense for you and your unique pregnancy, go for it.

Action Steps to Prepare for Birth

1. Read and learn: Find out everything you can about the different options available to you. Consult the reading list at the end of the book for some options.

2. Talk to your healthcare providers: Interview hospitals and doctors to find a good match. Find out what they recommend for your unique pregnancy.

3. Make a birth plan: Detail whether you want such interventions as continuous fetal heart monitoring or an epidural. Give it to the healthcare professionals who will attend you, whether that's a midwife or obstetrician. Share it with your partner and family.

4. Prepare to change the plan: Remind yourself that the birth plan is only that: a plan. It may need to be changed as labor progresses. The most important thing is that mother and baby stay well.

What If I Need a Cesarean?

Many women feel fear and grief when they find out they need to have a cesarean. It's certainly a more dangerous procedure than vaginal childbirth, and it's less than ideal for Oxytocin Parenting.

But, if your doctor recommends this for the health and safety of you and your baby, you should listen.

The best thing you can do as an Oxytocin Parent is to accept the need for this procedure as calmly as you can, remaining positive and focusing on the moment when you first hold your new baby in your arms. Remember, anxiety and fear are the result of stress chemicals flowing through your veins. These stress chemicals also communicate anxiety and fear to your baby.

Remind yourself that having a C-section is one of the many things you are doing to give your baby the best possible start in life.

It will not prevent you from bonding with your baby, and it won't harm his ability to learn the oxytocin response.

Chapter 16: Top Positive Parenting Qualities All Parents Should Possess

There is no sure-fire way to raise a perfect child. The way your kids turn out depends a lot on your personality and how your unique qualities play into the way your child and you interact. The positive impact you can have on your child is monumental, but first, you must learn to function with a positive mindset so that you can demonstrate positive traits such as a willingness to help others, generosity, empathy, standing up for one's beliefs, self-confidence, respect, etc.

We all have our strengths and weaknesses. But there are a number of strengths that consistently make positive parenting easier. To be a great parent, here are some of the qualities you need to possess in order to keep your child on a positive track.

1. Let it Go
It is a bitter reality, but sometimes you have to simply let go of your own feelings when you are dealing with a child. Sometimes, a child may hurt your feelings so deeply that you feel you may never get over it but you have to think out of the box. You have to become dispensable to many events, many heartaches, in order to practice effective positive parenting.

Encourage your kids to solve their own problems to give them confidence and allow them to discover their own abilities and skills. Many parents think that the child is little and won't be able to handle the situation on their own, but this only works to teach the child he is incapable of handling critical situations. If they are not given the chance to test their own abilities, when they are forced to handle a situation on their own, they won't be prepared and instead of acting in confidence they will panic. So it is always better to let kids learn on their own through their mistakes and guide them as best as you can.

You cannot impose your opinions on a child, but you can offer guidance. Ultimately you have to allow them to make their own mistakes. The child will repeat the mistake once or twice, and then the third time, he/she will be able to comprehend where he/she went wrong. Teach him/her the right way to deal with problems using critical thinking and observation which looks at the obstacle from each aspect.

It is never easy for parents to see their child in the midst of a problem. They wish they could take all the pain away, but their children will not learn from their mistakes if they do. Keep strong, knowing it will be harder for your child to deal with worldly matters when you are not there for them if you always step in and save them. So for their sake, you have to take a step back when your child is young and encourage him/her to handle their matters on their own.

2. Keep Your Marriage Strong

When the relationship between husband and wife is strong, they both work together for the healthy growth of their child mentally and physically. When both parents are able to get along with each other, it automatically reflects a positive attitude for the child. In this environment, a child will pick up the same positive attitude quickly and often have strong relationships as well. If the parent's relationship is not strong then it does have an adverse effect on the child mentally. Children raised in an environment where their parents do not have a strong relationship tend to be impatient and do not pay attention to others. When they grow up, they tend to be harsh communicators with those around them. Happy parents create a positive environment in the house which makes the kid patient, hopeful and attentive at the same time.

When the child watches his/her parents getting along and talking to each other with respect, then he/she grasps this quality and will often adopt this attitude for the rest of their life. There can be arguments between the parents at times, but you do not have to expose your child to your fights. Have difficult or emotionally charged conversations behind closed doors away from your child. The child should only know that his/her parents love each other and deal with each other with complete respect at all times.

3. Find Time for Fun

If you want to be great parents, then take time to have fun with your child. Having fun is also an opportunity for kids to learn because at a young age they can explore the world while being playful at the same time. Be playful with your child and entertain them the way he/she likes. Embrace the child and his/her joy by playing a complete part in it. So basically, become a kid yourself if you really want to enjoy your little one. These small activities play a vital role in the life of a child and their future, and it also enhances the attachment children have to their parents.

Plan a fun game, like a soccer match with your little one. Notice how much he/she enjoys defeating you and how that helps build their confidence. Providing toys for your kids so they can play on their own takes the joy out of spending time together doing activities your kids love. Playing together not only allows the child to feel a part of something important and helps them learn to interact in a healthy way, it also strengthens the parent-child bond and makes the child feel good about themselves and their place in the family.

4. Know How and When to Say No

Some parents say "no" for everything which leads to tough behavior on the part of a frustrated and angry child. The threatening nature of parents can lead to bad consequences for a child in the future. You need to know when it is appropriate to say no and how you have to convey that message to your child. If you talk in a harsh tone, then expect the same tone to come from the child, if not right away, then at some point down the road. You have to keep your authority as well as be friendly when your child insists on something. For example if a kid keeps insisting on watching TV late at night then you can say "We will watch TV together till late on the weekend." This way, the child is given a positive response and can look forward to watching TV with you when the weekend comes.

Certain rules need to be set by parents in order to discipline their children. Compromising on rules you have already set in place is not a way to build strong discipline. However, you can be flexible in your decisions regarding things your child asks for rather than always giving them a direct "no." Constantly saying "no" to your child will only encourage them to go behind your back (or lie) and do what they want anyways, because they know you will always say "no" to their request.

5. Be a Role Model

You have to play the role of the ideal person in your child's life where your child can look up to you and think "I want to be just like my mother or father." It takes a lot to be a role model for your child, but acting out of kindness is a great way to start. If you want your kids to be responsible and kind, then show them instead of telling them what to do all the time. They will be able to learn more by watching you than hearing verbal commands. If you tell your kids to be respectful to elders and you are not doing the same, then the kid will never listen to you unless he/she sees you doing the same as a parent. You have to provide guidance as a parent and do things which demonstrate a positive example for your kids to follow.

All the good things in life are positive. You can raise your child with the easy approach of positive parenting by modifying yourself along the way as well. If you know that you have been dealing with things without patience, then it is time that you start showing your patience. If you struggle with always raising your voice, find a way to better control your temper. Making changes to your own personality to become a great role model will have a positive effect on your child not only now, but in the future as well.

6. Endless Love

Love is something every parent feels when it comes to their children, but everyone expresses love differently. Some parents hide their love and never express it, whereas others shower their child with love on a constant basis. The second option is always the best – show love to your children. Never make your children feel that you are angry with them or not talking to them because they have made a mistake or made you angry in some way. You have to be forgiving and show affection whenever your child talks to you.

Do not have unrealistic expectations for your child. Keep in mind they are younger than you and know less than you know about the world. The smallest act of love you can give your child is your smile, and it can fill their day with happiness. So do not be grumpy if your child is not listening to you. Instead make him/her understand why you want them to listen and show them that everything you do for them is out of love.

Chapter 17: Do Not Set Your Expectations Too High

When you are new to the blended family situation, it is important to not expect everything to fall in place easily. The divorce did not happen overnight; and when it did happen, the children had a plethora of feelings about the way their lives were changing. Even considering the fighting and unhappiness between their parents, they have had the rug pulled out from under their world.

They have just either lost a parent from their home, or they have left behind a parent and have moved to another place. They need to heal and learn a whole new life without one of their parents being there all the time. Maybe they have finally gotten used to seeing both parents at different times and at different places.

If one of their parents passed away, then they will have spent some time mourning the parent and getting used to life without him/her. Now all of a sudden, the parent starts dating and trying to find someone new to be a partner and to share his/her life with that person. Here come more changes again!

So many adults just concentrate on the partnership without really considering the feelings of the children. We as adults tend to think that if we like someone, so will the other people in our lives because they love us and want us to be happy. How many children are really concerned with wanting their parents to be happy? Children, especially small ones, are mostly concerned with their own needs and wants.

When we fall in love with another person, we want to love everything about him or her, especially his/her family. When we consider a partner with a child or children, we want those kids to love us too. We believe that they will see how much we love their parent, and we naturally expect them to love us instantly.

This rarely happens. It takes time to build a strong relationship. Don't expect for it to just happen. In fact, it may never happen. When you go into this kind of a relationship, do not set your goals too high.

Strive toward being a nice person that they can like. Be kind and helpful and supportive. Strive for them just liking you. That is a great start. When they know that you like them, they will start to trust you—especially if you are consistent with them. Respect and love will follow when they know that you are sincere and that you are there for them.

Chapter 18: Positive Parenting With Young Children

It is quite scary as a parent, seeing your toddler walking and talking and making their own decisions. It means that they are growing up, and I can tell you there is no slowing down from this point forward. This chapter discusses major objectives that you as a parent should be covering as far as discipline and creating a well-rounded young adult go.

Giving Choices

Providing your child with the opportunities to make their own choices is one of the most imperative things a parent can do for their kids. This is a tool they will need to adequately manage their lives later on.

Limit choices by making them as agreeable as you can and crossing off any choices that you don't find acceptable.

Either/Or choices work the best with most children:

"We need to leave. Do you want to put on your shoes or would you like me to put them on for you?"

"If you want, you can quit basketball, but what other sports would you like to try? I want you to choose at least one physical activity."

Choices are tools that you can utilize to allow your kids to manage themselves.

"Once your homework is complete, I can help you carve a pumpkin. You can dawdle if you want, but I know how excited you are to carve that pumpkin."

In this scenario, they have the choice to either just do their homework or procrastinate, but you as a parent are motivating them to tackle the issue head on right away.

Choices are adequate methods in teaching children consequences.

"You have a piano recital coming up soon. If you practice extra, you will feel more confident playing, but that is your choice."

Don't offer children choices that you yourself cannot live with. If you are not so willing to allow your child to look like a fool at a recital, perhaps assist them with creating a structured practicing plan.

Empathy makes choices more effective. If children feel more understood, they will become less resistant and/or upset. This means they will usually make the right choice and move on from the situation.

Setting Limitations

Children of all ages need some sort of boundaries to live precariously by. Many parents absolutely loathe having to set limits for their children, which is where many things can go terribly wrong. But limits teach kids how to set boundaries for themselves in their own lives, which is a great tool in teaching self-discipline.

Set limits with empathy in mind

Begin with a supportive connection to your kid so they don't think you are living against them.

Look at things from their point of view and offer empathy that is truly genuine as you set limits.

Resist the temptation to allow your kid to get away with things, even small things.

Setting and sticking to limits teaches a lesson.

Only set limits when they really need set, so that the child still has plenty of opportunity to discover things on their own and learn from them. Saying no too often can hurt the child, especially in their later years.

Limit behavior but allow feelings. Children are allowed to have their feelings, just like adults do. It is a natural reaction for them to feel anger when we set a boundary. The job of a parent is to accept the way they feel and love them through that situation. If you react to your child's tantrums without any empathy, he/she learns that feeling the way they do is unacceptable.

Chapter 19: In A Nutshell

You have the resources to do whatever you want to do.

This is all about:

* believing that you DO have the skill you need,

* asking yourself, "What is the skill I need,"

* and then, "When and where do I have this skill?"

* what is the structure of this skill, how do I do what I do well?

* do it!

Personal note from me…

How often do we shrug off compliments saying, "it was nothing" and beat ourselves up over the things we think we don't do well, thinking that everyone else can do it better?

How do our kids learn confidence if we show them this pattern?

Personal note to yourself…

3. If someone else can do it you can too

This is a very empowering belief.

How often do we see other parents do things that we admire and would like to do ourselves?

We already have the resources as we learned in the last chapter but what if it's a completely new skill or a refinement of a skill we already have?

If you have noticed a skill in someone else, the chances are that in some way you too have this skill because that is how you come to have noticed it in the first place.

We say, "If you spot it, you've got it!"

You can acquire these new skills and hone existing ones by modelling (or copying) it in someone who demonstrates that skill with excellence.

This is an excellent tool to teach children. Your child knows who in their class is best at their times tables, spelling, singing, acting, drawing and so on. Learn how to model so you can teach them to get the skills they want from other children they know.

Use it to pass on your skills to them too.

How do we do it?

a) First we need to identify the skill we want.

We do this by observation. Observe and be intently curious about what you see and how your model (the person you want the skill from) behaves.

Watch every part of the skill, the non-verbal cues such as body language and the verbal ones, the tone of voice, language patterns, volume and pace.

What you're looking for is –

"I want to model the way x (the person) does y (the skill)"

If you've never done this before, start with something small such as how to make something, how to spell a word, remember a phone number, use a particular computer programme or do something in the gym. Then move on to something bigger once you're familiar with the process.

Identify which part of the skill you need because it is unlikely you need all of it.

Then break it into small parts that you can practice.

For example, let's say your child is having problems making friends at their new school. This is quite a big 'chunk' and can seem overwhelming to a child. Ask them what exactly they'd like to be able to do. Maybe what they want is the courage to go up to someone they don't know. I expect you do this all the time so you can talk them through how you do it and pass on the skill.

B) Think about the belief your model would have in order to use that skill.

Do this by reflecting 'If I did that I would be thinking I was... ' Perhaps your model sounds confident or calm, controlled or firm?

Where in your life do you have that belief?

Maybe you have that belief when you are at work, with your friends or at the gym?

Think hard about where you have the belief and visualize yourself in that situation where the belief is strong.

If you're passing on the skill to a child, ask them when and where they have the skill they need.

In the earlier example perhaps they are able to approach people they don't know in other circumstances such as asking for the toilet at someone's birthday party.

Have you left some of your work skills at work?

It's not unusual for parents to forget about the things they did well when they were working.

Even if you are a 'stay at home' mum or dad or are doing a different job now that you have children, those skills are still part of your repertoire and may need to be brought into your parenting role. So dust off that skill and belief so that you have them now in your parenting role.

When you use NLP with your children it is very useful to be able to show them where they have skills that you observe at home, so that they can take them into school along with the underlying belief about having the skill.

Now practice the precise skill you have identified. You can do this on your own first and then practice on the family.

Notice what results you get and keep practicing until you get your desired outcome.

You may find that you need more models of that skill so you can observe different executions of it. Talk to the models about how they do it and what they believe about the way they do it. It often takes a few different models of a skill to help you acquire it for yourself and use in a way that works for you.

Once you have mastered this modelling exercise you can show your children how to do it.

A good way for children to get a skill is to ask, "How do you do that?" and then, "Can you show me how to do it?" It's a really good way of making friends too.

Remember that you are a natural model for your children because they are observing you every day and will unconsciously be modelling you and those you interact with regularly.

If your children are doing something you don't like; you may need to check that you aren't unconsciously modelling this behaviour yourself. It may not be an exact copy but ask yourself, "When do I do this?"

How often do we hear a child sounding just like one of their parents?

We laugh when they come out with an expression or mannerism we have, so you need to model the behaviour you want from them rather than what you don't want.

You may need to demonstrate a skill quite deliberately to make a point even saying, "Watch how mummy (or daddy) does this."

If you are having food issues with your children not eating what you've cooked; then eat with them because when you show them how you eat that thing, it encourages them to copy you.

Involve your partner because they are important role models, especially for boys. Teachers will often observe how boys who are poor readers have dads who don't read in their child's presence.

Use modelling skills as part of your on-going personal development and show your children how to follow your lead.

There are plenty of things children do that are great for you to model too. Children are real experts in being fully present. They tend not to worry about the future but absorb themselves in what they are doing right now, playing Lego or kicking a ball around, playing with dolls. This enables them to be in the here and now which is a good place for us to be for our mental health.

Children are very observant and they're good at being 'in the moment', 'being present' and enjoying what they are doing right now. That's why they don't want to do what you've asked them possibly.

How often do we think only about what we have to do next rather than enjoying what we are doing right now?

Chapter 20: Don't Program Your Child With Negative Rubbish

Do you recognize this conversation, "All of my friends are allowed to watch it." We've all heard this argument, but you as the parents have the responsibility to decide what you want to expose your child to. Violence in schools and in society in general has increased greatly over the years and studies are showing a link between media viewing and violence in teenagers. In fact, children who watch violence on TV at the age of five are twice as likely to develop teen aggression.

Parents of young children need to train their children to watch appropriate and educational programs because studies also show that preschool children who watch documentaries and information programs achieve higher results in high school English, Math and Science. There are many fantastic programs available for young children, you can record these and play at a later date.

Programs that encourage children to be cheeky and speak badly to other people should also be avoided. The less exposure your child has to bad attitudes and poor manners the better. Don't let young children watch programs like The Simpsons, it will only teach them how to be cheeky and disrespectful.

When our children were toddlers and displaying negative behaviors, we would sit down with them and put on a Barney DVD. Barney is a purple dinosaur and the videos are about different positive values and personal characteristics. By the end of the DVD our children would be singing the Barney song and happy again. Then we would talk about their previous behavior and why it is much better to be pleasant and happy.

As your child enters Primary or Elementary School they will want to watch the programs their friends are viewing and play a bigger variety of games on Playstation and X Box. View the programs and games first. You can borrow the games from a video store overnight and check them out before buying. Make sure you look at the rating on the game to ensure it is suitable for your child's age group.

Don't use the TV as a babysitter. Sit down as a family and watch TV together. You can even talk about the commercials and discuss how they are trying to influence people. Talk about different cultures you see on TV and also problems that people face and how they can solve them. Make TV viewing an interesting time.

Chapter 21: Communication And Environment

In addition to encouraging a sense of community outside of the home, you also need to provide the right environment inside of your home. It is your job as a parent to provide a positive place for your children to live. It is important to avoid excessive negativity especially in any interactions you have with your child.

There are many ways a negative situation can happen and sometimes they just can't be avoided. How we respond is key to keeping the experience positive and something to learn from.

You may, however, be predisposed to be a negative person in the way your think and respond. This will require some adjustment to your mindset in order to be a more positive parent.

Analyzing your Behavior First

How do you know if you have a tendency to be negative? Ask yourself the following questions:

Do you react negatively in most situations?

Think about an example of a negative situation in your life. How did you react? Why did you react in that manner?

What are at least three other ways you could have reacted better that would have been more positive?

The next time that situation occurs, choose to stop, think, and then use one of the more positive reactions.

If you can get into this thinking cycle, then you are going to have more success in creating a positive environment.

Removing Negatives

There are many situations that can set you up to be more likely to react in a negative way (remember how we talked about being hungry or tired?).

Here is an example:

A grandfather would always say "oh [expletive!]" every time he dropped something. A baby who observed and listened to everything he said then used that curse word whenever she dropped something - it happened to be her first word! Now the child has gotten used to saying the word even in front of adults because they think it is funny. When the parents laugh, they encouraged the child rather than correcting.

To be a positive parent, you have to be able to correct or even discipline your child without being negative. You have to remember that correcting your child is not punishment, it is actually a way of showing love through teaching and guidance.

Don't be the parent who says "do as I say and not as I do." For one, it sets a bad example and is confusing. Secondly, your child will find it difficult not to follow your example especially when they are younger.

To be a positive parent, you must remove the negative influences or at least limit them. You must also be willing to change your own habits and reactions to be positive and rewarded when needed.

Above all else, don't forget that love in the form of words, hugs, and kisses are not only for when your child is good. Love should be given at all times and is essential to showing your child the importance of the lessons you have taught them. Love should be used to reinforce those lessons, not to punish. Poor behavior needs love and affection as much as good behavior does

Chapter 22: Fixing A Child's Behavior

Threatening to provide consequences for an inappropriate action doesn't provide a good learning tool for a toddler. It can teach the child to avoid one situation to sidestep another situation. The child has to understand when the behavior is not tolerable. Parents also need to be a role model and teach the child. With that said, you also have to realize children learn from other children. You need to address the child's needs and not his/her behavior to get the ball rolling.

The coin is two-sided, meaning you are reacting if the child has made a mess (you will need to clean up), such as playing the sugar dish on the dining room table. You need to understand maybe the child might like the way it cascades onto the table or the feel of the grits that are so similar to sand on the beach. You never know what the toddler is thinking.

You have a choice. You need to eliminate the problem by asking the toddler if he/she understands this is not a good thing. Distraction can also be a tool used when a child is acting out. If the child is throwing toys all over the house, make it a game of who can fill the toy basket first. Reverse psychology works well with most children. Make the task fun and your child will probably follow suit and help.

The foremost objective is to provide an alternative for the child. Suggest another activity such as coloring a picture— supervised – of course. If you have a swing set in the yard or a park close by, go for a change of scenery.

Identify the Child's Feelings

Frustration can ensue if you or your child becomes angry or combative. If the child is playing with other youngsters and he/she believes it is time for him/her to use the item, an argument could be in the making. Teaching a child to share can be difficult on a good day but providing an alternative is always helpful.

Let the child throw a bit of a fit if he/she believes it is necessary. It might take a couple of minutes for the child to calm back down, but you can help the child understand why it is not appropriate behavior. Suggest another activity so the child doesn't feel so threatened.

Solve the Trigger

If you are in full-blown anxiety mode and don't know what to do, take a moment to regroup. Asking why a child acted out or why he/she got angry is not effective through the moments of anger. You need to discover what caused or triggered the outburst.

For example, if your child destroyed a sibling's toy, you need to find the root to the problem. Was it because of jealousy or other situations? For a toddler, it can be difficult to choose a starting point. A process of elimination will benefit you and the child for any events that could be triggered from the same source at a later time if the problem isn't solved.

You cannot allow the child to rule the situation. Even toddlers need to learn life sometimes just isn't fair and adjustments need to be made that don't always go with your original plan. You have to shift your thinking and focus on what the child is thinking.

To change the behavior, you have to leave the emotional baggage behind. You can't make excuses on the reaction of the child. You have to find a way to reason with the youngster, so he/she understands the behavior is bad or isn't acceptable.

Bribery Does Not Work

Some days, parents have used all of the day's patience and sanity—which is normal—when you are working with a toddler and his or her pesky behaviors. Don't use bribery as a tool to get a positive reaction from your child because it could be a sign the behavior is acceptable.

It is best to stop what you are doing and see if your child wants to play a new game or just go outside and play. Boredom can start much of the stress involved with behavioral issues. As your child gets older, the bribery method will become a way to get treats even when they aren't necessary or advisable.

Good Rewards for Good Behavior

Training a child with a good reward system is excellent once you have a pattern. The use of a timer is a good way for your toddler to learn responsibilities. Give your child a set time to do a task and show him/her where the dial will be when the time is up.

For many years, the older school systems used a star system for good behavior. Take a chapter out of that book for your toddler. Make a chart and let the child know when it is full of stars, he/she can select a special treat from the choices you provide.

The system will work best for toddlers, but it could take a couple of months before you receive the results you desire. Choose one or two flaws your child needs to work on, such as picking up toys or getting ready for bed when asked to do so.

The star system is a great learning tool which can be used to tally and relay good deeds to your child. If you observe the child playing quietly, putting toys away, or any similar actions—it is time for a star. If the child misbehaves during the star-time, a star will be lost. Your child will notice when a star disappears.

Quiet Time

Set small goals for your toddler with a quiet recess for him/her to play in the play room or bedroom. Begin with thirty-minute increments but still check on the child often. As the behavior modifies, try increasing quiet time. The quiet goals give the child time to use his/her talents to learn how to play independently. This time is not the same as a time-out.

Chapter 23: Make Them Feel Special And Loved

Every child is unique and you know your child is special because he is yours. However, he might not realize this yet. So, it's important that you make every effort to make him feel that he is exceptional in every way. Children tend to feel responsible when things go wrong, and during difficult events like the divorce of their parents or the death of a sibling, they have a tendency to feel that it may be their fault. You have to make sure you reassure your children that adult decisions and issues are not their fault. It's important to explain to the child that they should also not feel guilty if an accident happens. In the event of one of these situations happening, they should be comforted and listened to. Of course, you should not wait until difficult events to make your little one feel special. This should be your mission on a daily basis. Also, parents are usually pretty good about buying chocolate on Easter and lots of presents at Christmas, but be sure not to wait until there is a special occasion to make your little one feel special. And it's important to understand that gifts and material things are not what makes your child feel most special. Your undivided attention and unexpected little thoughts and gestures will be the best gift that makes him feel most loved.

There are many examples of little things you can do to make your child feel special and loved. Leave a cute note or a joke in their lunch box, or surprise them with story time in the middle of the day. In the morning when you wake your child up, allow yourself an additional 5 or 10 minutes once in a while to have tickle fight. On the weekends, play restaurant, and allow your child to order breakfast. Take his order, cook the eggs, pancakes, waffles or whatever he chose and serve him breakfast on the couch while allowing him to watch his favorite cartoons. Once in a while, for no reason, break the rules. Allow your child to stay up an additional 30 minutes. Perhaps on a week night you could make popcorn and put in a movie and watch it together, something you usually do only on weekends. Pay your child a visit at school and bring lunch for the both of you. Not only can you be certain your daughter or son will be excited to introduce you to his friends and teacher, but you can also check out what's going on in his school life. Have their towels embroidered with their names or create cute labels for them when they go off for the weekend to their first Boy Scout camp. Instead of watching him jump at one of those trampoline centers, dress comfortably and join him! Its great exercise and a few hours of guaranteed fun. Watch them when they are riding their bikes outside or decorating their cupcakes so carefully. All of these things are very small in reality, but very large in their mind.

Making your children feel special is telling them they are loved. Boosting their self-confidence will help them tremendously in life. They will have a better chance at succeeding in sports, at school or at any other hobbies or activities they will undertake. If you have established a solid relationship of trust between the two of you, your child will truly believe how special they are. This might also give them additional motivation to try new things or simply perform everything they try to the very best of their ability. Always make sure, however, that your child knows that even if he is struggling in a subject at school or he is having a hard time staying within the lines when coloring, he has other talents. It is important to not expect perfection from your child, but to teach them to simply do their best.

Chapter 24: Software Recommendation For Children Of Different Ages

Here are some of my recommended applications for children of different ages. Although new applications may have developed over the years, I am focusing on the objective of what they can achieve for our kids.

1- to 2-year-olds

For 1- to 2-year-old children, games with random animations and sound effects that are applied when a random touch is done are more suitable for them, since these children have a higher chance of doing random touching.

Fun for Kids - Puzzles

Every time a puzzle is finished, a fun song or tune is played. With lots of puzzles, colorful graphics, and different difficulty levels, your toddler will develop problem-solving and motor skills while enjoying the game all at the same time.

Talking Pocoyo and Talking Cat

If you have a toddler you may have encountered these apps titled **Talking Pocoyo** or **Talking Ginger Cat** and **Talking Tom Cat**. These games will help your toddler engage in communication and interact with it by talking. Animations appear every time they touch any part of the character to keep them fully entertained.

Fruit Ninja

Colorful fruits in HD quality bounce around the screen and are sliced in half by a swiping motion. It has a beautiful background sound and sound effects that increase the enjoyment and interest of children. This game in particular will help your toddler develop and strengthen their hand and eye coordination.

3- to 5-year-olds

For children whose age ranges from 3 to 5, applications like teaching them how to sing and pronounce words, memorize the alphabet, the names of colors and numbers are now applicable to them.

Conclusion

After reading this book you have realized where you have been going wrong in raising your preschooler. You have known thing you have not been doing and it is not too late.

With time you will realize that if your kids were afraid of you they will start opening up. This is because your game will have upped. The relationship with them will increase drastically and their faces will be forever bright.

You will also realize that you will experience an inner joy that comes with good parenting tips. You will find parenting easy and fun. In fact, parents without the knowledge you have acquired from this book will come for your advice.

You will also be amazed by how your youngster will love school. It goes without saying that if a youngster loves school, then there is a high probability that her performance will be good. The two things go hand in hand.

I wish you all the best as you make parenting interesting and raise adorable children. Adios amigo J

www.ingramcontent.com/pod-product-compliance
Lightning Source LLC
Chambersburg PA
CBHW072008070526
44583CB00015B/1390